Mushroom

Barrie Watts

Stopwatch books

 Silver Burdett Company • Morristown, New Jersey

These mushrooms are good to eat.

Have you ever eaten mushrooms like these? Look at their different shapes. Some are button mushrooms and some are flat mushrooms.

Here are a button mushroom and a flat mushroom.

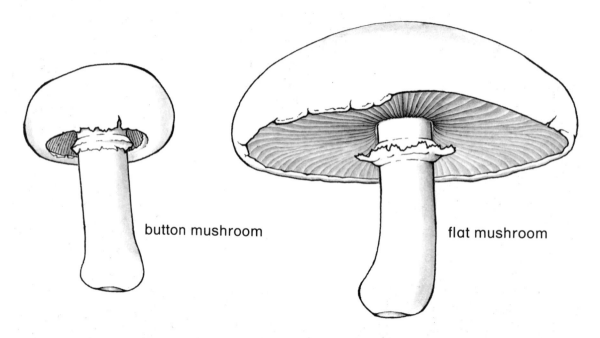

button mushroom

flat mushroom

The button mushroom was picked when it was young.
The flat mushroom was picked when it was older.
It has grown bigger than the button mushroom.

This book shows you how a mushroom grows.

This is where mushrooms grow.

These wild mushrooms are growing in a field.

Wild mushrooms come up once a year. You can find them in early autumn when the weather is warm and damp. Never eat them unless a grownup says they are all right.

Look at the big photograph. These mushrooms are growing on a special mushroom farm. They can grow here all year round. The mushrooms we eat usually come from mushroom farms like this one.

The mushroom has a stalk and a cap.

Here is a mushroom growing in the soil. The bottom part of the mushroom is called the stalk. On top of the stalk is the cap. The cap is shaped a bit like an umbrella.

You can't see all of the mushroom in this photograph. Part of it grows under the ground, like this.

The stalk is joined to little threads in the ground. The threads take in water and food from the soil. The mushroom needs food and water to live.

Under the cap there are gills.

Underneath the mushroom cap there are lots of thin flaps.
They are called gills. Look at the big photograph.
The gills are dark brown. They are covered in tiny
brown specks, called spores.

You can't see the spores in the photograph. But if you
put a mushroom cap down on a piece of paper, some of
the spores will drop out, like this.

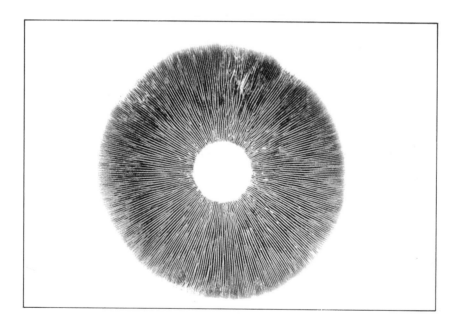

The pattern which they make is called a spore print.

Spores grow on the gills.

This mushroom cap has been cut down the middle.
Can you see the brown gill? It is covered with spores.
Thousands of spores can grow on each gill.

This picture shows the spores very large.

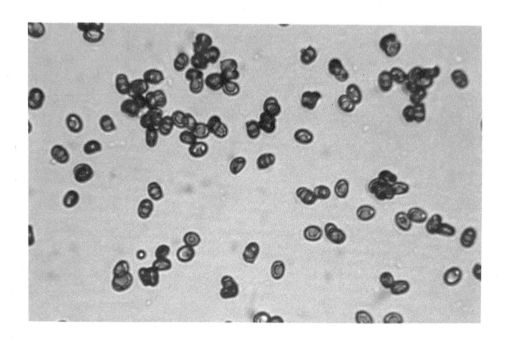

In real life, thousands and thousands of these tiny
spores would fit onto the head of a pin.

When the spores are fully grown, they fall off the gills.

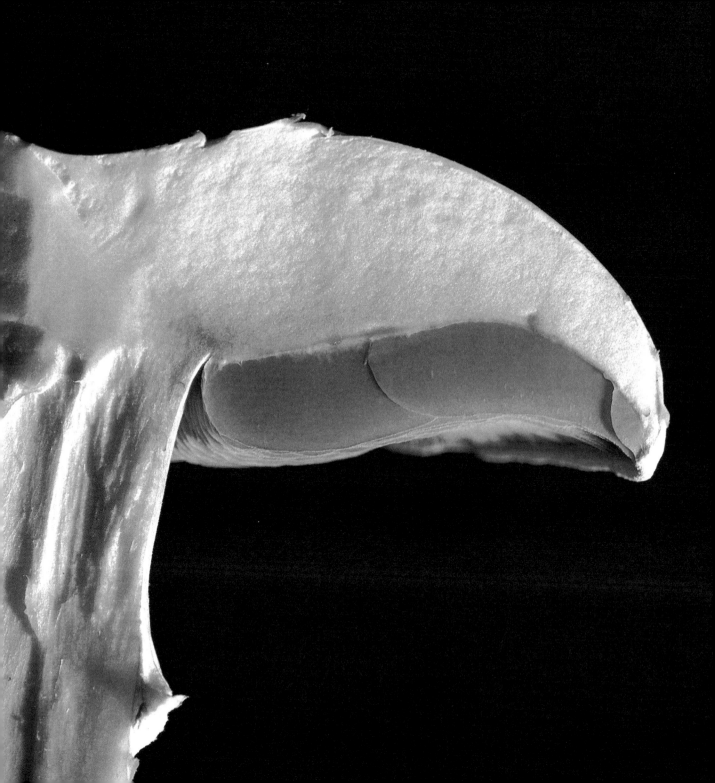

Threads grow from the spores.

The spores are very light so the wind carries them away from the mushroom.

Sometimes a spore lands on damp soil. Then tiny threads come out from the spore, like this.

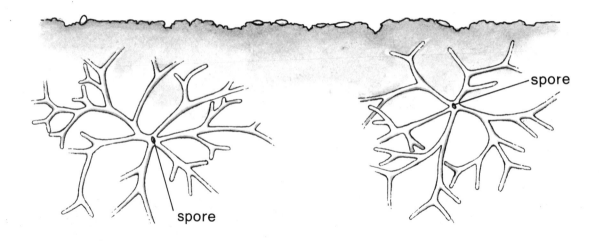

spore

spore

Look at the photograph. The threads are growing. They look a bit like cotton thread.

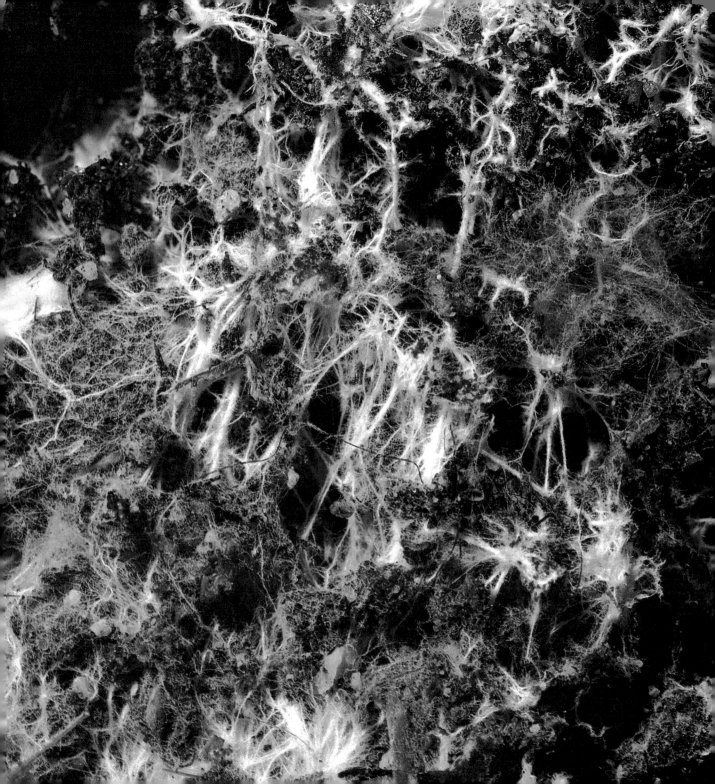

A new mushroom grows from the threads.

Sometimes two threads meet in the soil. Then a mushroom starts to grow. Look at the drawing.

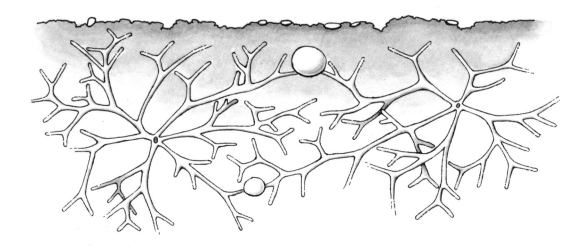

Where two threads join there is a bump. Soon the bump swells up into a button. This will be a new mushroom.

Look at the photograph. Can you see the new mushroom? There are other new mushrooms growing nearby. They are pushing up through the soil.

The mushroom grows above the ground.

If the weather is warm and damp the mushroom grows very quickly. In one day it can double in size.

Here is the mushroom cut down the middle.

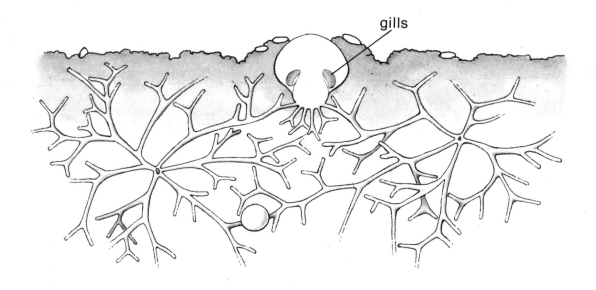

gills

Can you see the gills growing inside it?

Look at the photograph. The mushroom has pushed up through the top of the soil.

The cap breaks away from the stalk.

Look at the drawing. Can you see where the outside of the cap is joined to the stalk?

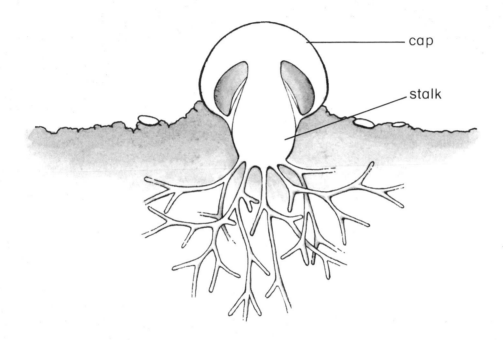

cap

stalk

As the button mushroom swells up, the cap breaks away from the stalk. Some of the cap is left on the stalk. This is called the ring.

Now look at the photograph. Can you see the ring on this mushroom?

The cap gets flatter.

Now the mushroom cap is almost flat. If you look under the cap you can see the gills.

At first the gills are pink. But they soon turn brown. Look at the big photograph. Spores are growing on the gills.

The mushroom is old.

Slugs and snails like to eat mushrooms. They make holes in the mushroom cap.

Soon the mushroom gets old and dry. Its spores blow away in the wind. Some of the spores will land on warm damp soil. What do you think will happen to them?

Do you remember how a mushroom grows?
See if you can tell the story in your own words.
You can use these pictures to help you.

Index

3

6

This index will help you to find some of the important words in the book.

Gently put a mushroom cap with the gills facing downward on a piece of white paper. Leave it overnight. When you lift the cap you will have a spore print.
Never pick and eat mushrooms unless you are with a grownup.